INSIDER SECRETS AND PRACTICAL
ADVICE FOR GROWING YOU
BEER, WINE, OR SPIRIT BRAND

LAUNCHING YOUR
ALCOHOL
BRAND
IN THE U.S.

DAVE MOORE

Contents

Preface

As a seasoned veteran of the wine industry with over two decades of experience, I've had the privilege of working with some of the most renowned brands and distributors in the United States. Throughout my journey, I've witnessed firsthand the challenges and opportunities that come with navigating the complex three-tier distribution system.

When I first entered the world of wine in 2002, I was immediately drawn to its complexity and romance. From the intricacies of winemaking to the rich history and geography behind each bottle, I knew I had found my calling. As I progressed in my career, taking on strategic roles at companies like Southern Glazers Wine & Spirits and Young's Market Company (Republic National Distributing Company), I developed a deep understanding of the business side of the industry.

My experience as the general manager of Schug Winery in Sonoma, California, was a pivotal moment in my career. Leading the revitalization of this iconic brand, I realized the importance of strong relationships, effective brand strategies, and a thorough understanding of the distribution landscape. It was during this time that I recognized the need for a comprehensive resource to guide entrepreneurs and new entrants in the alcohol industry.

Launching Your Alcohol Brand in the U.S. is the culmination of my passion for the industry and my desire to share the knowledge

I've gained over the years. This book is designed to empower startups and small brands with the tools and insights they need to succeed in the world's largest alcohol consumer market.

Whether you're a craft brewer, a boutique winery, or an artisan distiller, the strategies and advice in this book will help you navigate the challenges of the three-tier system, forge strong relationships with distributors, and ultimately grow your brand.

Writing this book has been a personal challenge and a fulfilling experience. It has allowed me to reflect on the lessons I've learned, the relationships I've built, and the incredible journey that the alcohol industry has taken me on. I hope that by sharing my insights I can inspire and guide you, the next generation of entrepreneurs, as you embark on your own journeys in this dynamic and rewarding industry.

INTRODUCTION

Welcome to *Launching Your Alcohol Brand in the U.S.: A Guide for Startups Navigating the Three-Tier System – Insider Secrets and Practical Advice for Growing Your Beer, Wine, or Spirits Brand.* As a seasoned professional with over two decades of experience in the alcohol industry, I'm excited to share my knowledge and insights to help you, as a startup or new entrant, master the unique challenges of the U.S. alcohol distribution landscape.

If you're a craft brewer, a boutique winery, or an artisan distiller looking to launch your first product or expand your brand's presence in the United States, this book is for you. Navigating the complex three-tier system can be daunting without the right guidance, but with the strategies and insights shared in this book you'll be well-equipped to build a successful brand in the world's largest alcohol consumer market.

Drawing from my extensive experience working with major distributors and managing a family-owned winery, I've distilled my industry knowledge into actionable strategies to help you thrive within the three-tier system. We'll dive into the history and purpose of this unique regulatory framework, which was established after Prohibition to ensure compliance, provide market access, promote fair competition, and facilitate efficient tax collection. Understanding the foundations of the three-tier system is crucial for developing effective strategies to build your brand.

Throughout this book, we'll explore each tier's role and dynamics, offering practical insights to help you forge strong relationships with distributors, maximize your product's potential, and navigate regulatory complexities with confidence. You'll gain the tools and knowledge needed to transform your understanding of the U.S. alcohol distribution landscape into tangible business growth.

While the primary focus of this book is on startups and new entrants, the principles and strategies outlined are valuable for established brands, distributors, and retailers as well. By providing a comprehensive view of the system and addressing common challenges, such as communication gaps between suppliers and distributors, this book aims to foster a more collaborative and efficient industry ecosystem.

Whether you're just starting out or looking to refine your approach, *Launching Your Alcohol Brand in the U.S.* is your guide to building a sustainable and profitable brand presence within the U.S. three-tier system. Let's embark on this journey together, as we explore the past, present, and future of alcohol distribution in America. With the right strategies and a deep understanding of the three-tier system, you'll be well-equipped to overcome challenges, seize opportunities, and achieve your brand's full potential in the United States.

CHAPTER 1

Understanding the Three-Tier System

1.1 Introduction

Welcome to the world of alcohol distribution in the United States. At the heart of this complex landscape lies the three-tier system, a regulatory framework that has shaped the industry since the end of Prohibition. In this chapter, we'll dive into the historical roots of the system, break down its structure, and explore the roles of each tier. We'll also navigate the complex web of regulations and compliance requirements that governs the system and examine how its implementation varies across states.

As someone who has worked in various roles within the alcohol industry, I've seen firsthand how understanding the three-tier system is crucial for success. Whether you're a craft whiskey looking to expand your distribution or a seasoned industry professional seeking to optimize your operations, having a deep grasp of this framework will empower you to make informed decisions and develop effective strategies.

So, let's dive in and gain a comprehensive understanding of the three-tier system and how to navigate it effectively.

1.2 Historical Context of the Three-Tier System

1.2.1 Origins and Rationale

To understand the three-tier system, we must first travel back in time to the era of Prohibition. From 1920 to 1933, the production, sale, and transportation of alcohol was banned in the United States. When Prohibition ended with the ratification of the 21st Amendment in 1933, policymakers sought to create a new regulatory framework that would address the issues that had plagued the alcohol industry before Prohibition, such as tied houses, monopolistic practices, and public health concerns.

The solution they devised was the three-tier system, which mandated a separation between alcohol producers, distributors, and retailers. By preventing vertical integration and promoting a fair, competitive market, the system aimed to ensure product safety, facilitate tax collection, and encourage responsible consumption.

1.2.2 Evolution and Challenges

Over the decades, the three-tier system has faced its share of challenges. Consolidation within the producer and distributor tiers has raised concerns about the system's ability to prevent monopolistic practices. The rise of the craft beverage movement has put pressure on the system to accommodate smaller producers. And the digital age, with its e-commerce platforms and direct-to-consumer (DTC) sales models, has challenged traditional distribution channels.

Despite these challenges, the three-tier system has shown remarkable resilience and adaptability. Recent adaptations have seen some states introduce limited exceptions for small producers, while the COVID-19 pandemic prompted temporary relaxations of certain regulations. As we explore the modern alcohol industry, understanding the historical context and ongoing evolution of the three-tier system remains crucial for navigating its complexities and adapting to new challenges.

1.3 Unveiling the Three Tiers

At its core, the three-tier system is designed to prevent monopolistic practices and ensure a fair, competitive market for alcohol sales. Let's take a closer look at each tier and the vital roles they play within the system.

1.3.1 Producers (First Tier)

Producers, which include breweries, distilleries, and wineries, are the creative force behind the alcohol industry. As a former manager of a family-owned winery, I know firsthand the passion and dedication that goes into crafting a unique product. However, under the three-tier system, producers are required to sell their products exclusively to wholesale distributors, rather than directly to retailers or consumers.

1.3.2 Distributors (Second Tier)

Distributors are the essential link between producers and retailers. Having worked for major distributors like Southern Glazer's Wine & Spirits (formerly Southern Wine & Spirits) and RNDC (Republic National Distributing Company, formerly Youngs Market Company), I've seen the critical role they play in ensuring compliance, managing inventory, and executing sales and marketing strategies. Distributors are responsible for getting the right products to the right retailers, all while navigating a complex web of state and local regulations.

1.3.3 Retailers (Third Tier)

Retailers, including bars, restaurants, and liquor stores, are the face of the alcohol industry to the consumer. They are tasked with responsibly selling alcohol while adhering to a host of regulations, from age verification to operating hour restrictions. Building strong relationships with retailers is key to the success of any alcohol brand.

1.3.4 Tier Interactions

One of the most important things I've learned in my years in the industry is that success in the three-tier system relies heavily on the interactions between the tiers. Producers depend on distributors for market access, distributors rely on producers for innovative products and on retailers for sales, and retailers depend on distributors for a steady supply of inventory. Navigating these interdependent relationships is both an art and a science, requiring a deep understanding of each tier's unique challenges and priorities.

1.4 Regulations and Compliance

Compliance with federal, state, and local regulations is a critical concern for every business operating within the three-tier system. From licensing and labeling to distribution laws and compliance monitoring, the regulatory landscape is vast and complex.

In my experience, investing in a robust compliance program is essential for long-term success. This means staying up to date on changing regulations, maintaining meticulous records, and fostering open communication with regulators and industry partners. It also means being proactive in adapting to emerging trends, such as the rise of e-commerce and DTC sales, which are challenging traditional regulatory models.

1.5 Variations across States

One of the most challenging aspects of the U.S. alcohol industry is the significant variation in how the three-tier system is implemented from state to state. From control states, where the government plays a direct role in distribution and retail, to license states with their patchwork of regulations, each jurisdiction presents its own unique set of opportunities and obstacles.

Throughout my career, I've learned that a one-size-fits-all approach rarely works in this industry. Successful alcohol brands must be nimble and adaptable, tailoring their strategies to the specific requirements of each state in which they operate. This means building a deep understanding of local market conditions, forging strong relationships with state-specific partners, and being prepared to pivot when necessary.

1.6 Conclusion

The three-tier system is not just a regulatory framework; it is a living, breathing ecosystem that shapes every aspect of the U.S. alcohol industry. From its post-Prohibition origins to its ongoing evolution in the face of new challenges and opportunities, the system remains the foundation upon which the industry is built.

As we've explored in this chapter, understanding the historical context, structure, and variations of the three-tier system is essential for anyone looking to build a successful alcohol brand in the United States. By embracing the complexities of this system and leveraging the unique insights and strategies I've shared, you'll be well-equipped to navigate the challenges and seize the opportunities that lie ahead.

In the next chapter, we'll dive deeper into the legal and regulatory landscape of the alcohol industry, exploring the specific laws and compliance requirements that impact each tier of the system. So, get ready to take notes, and let's continue our exploration of alcohol distribution in America and how to navigate it successfully.

CHAPTER 2

Navigating the Legal and Regulatory Landscape

Disclosure Statement: The information provided in this chapter and throughout this book is for general informational purposes only. It is not intended to be, and should not be construed as, legal advice. The author is not an attorney, compliance officer, or regulatory expert. Laws and regulations in the alcohol industry are complex and subject to change. Readers are strongly encouraged to consult with qualified legal professionals and compliance experts for specific advice relating to their particular situations and jurisdictions.

2.1 Introduction

Welcome to the intricate world of alcohol industry regulations. As we explored in Chapter 1, the three-tier system is the foundation of alcohol distribution in the United States. However, navigating this system successfully requires a deep understanding of the legal and regulatory landscape that governs it.

In my years of experience working with major distributors and managing small wineries, I've learned that a solid grasp of these regulations is not just a legal necessity—it's a crucial competitive advantage. By understanding the rules of the game, you can avoid costly pitfalls, seize opportunities others might miss, and build trust with regulators, partners, and customers alike.

In this chapter, we'll dive into the key aspects of federal and state regulations, explore recent legal changes and ongoing challenges, and discuss the importance of compliance. While the legal terrain can seem daunting at times, remember that every successful player in the alcohol industry has had to master these same challenges. With the right knowledge and strategies, you too can navigate this landscape with confidence and skill.

2.2 Overview of Federal Regulations

At the federal level, two main bodies oversee the alcohol industry: the Alcohol and Tobacco Tax and Trade Bureau (TTB) and the Food and Drug Administration (FDA).

The TTB is responsible for collecting taxes, ensuring proper labeling, and overseeing the production and distribution of alcohol. Key regulations enforced by the TTB include the Federal Alcohol Administration Act, which establishes basic permit requirements, as well as labeling, advertising, formulation, and production requirements.

The FDA, while playing a more limited role, oversees food safety regulations that apply to certain aspects of alcohol production and regulates the use of additives in alcohol products.

As someone who has worked closely with these federal agencies, I can attest to the importance of understanding and complying with their regulations. Whether you're a craft distillery seeking formula approval or a winery navigating labeling requirements, a proactive approach to federal compliance is essential.

2.3 State-Level Regulations—A Diver Landscape

While federal laws provide the overarching framework, state regulations add another layer of complexity. Each state has its own set of laws governing alcohol production, distribution, and sale, and these vary widely across the country.

Some key areas where state laws differ include DTC shipping, franchise laws, and "tied house" laws that affect how suppliers interact with retailers. Additionally, the distinction between control states, where the government controls some aspect of alcohol sales, and license states, where private businesses obtain licenses, significantly impacts how the three-tier system operates in each jurisdiction.

Throughout my career, I've seen firsthand how these state-level variations necessitate tailored strategies. What works in a license state like California may not be feasible in a control state like Pennsylvania. The key is to develop a deep understanding of each state's unique regulatory environment and adapt your approach accordingly.

2.4 Recent Legal Changes and Ongoing Challenges

The legal landscape of the alcohol industry is constantly evolving, with recent years witnessing significant changes and ongoing debates. The growth of e-commerce has sparked discussions about DTC sales and challenged traditional distribution models. Many states have revised their laws to accommodate the booming craft very industry, often allowing limited self-distribution rights. Ongoing discussions about interstate shipping laws continue to shape the regulatory environment, particularly for wineries.

As an industry professional, staying informed about these legal developments is crucial. Regularly engaging with industry associations, attending conferences, and following relevant publications can help you stay ahead of the curve. In my experience, being proactive in understanding and adapting to legal changes can open up new opportunities and give you a competitive edge.

2.5 Compliance–A Necessary Foundation for Success

Compliance with all applicable laws and regulations is not just a legal obligation—it's a business imperative. Noncompliance can result in fines, license suspensions, or even criminal charges, all of which can be devastating to your brand and your reputation.

To build a strong foundation of compliance, consider the following strategies:

- **Review:** Regularly review and update your compliance procedures to ensure that they align with the latest regulations.

- **Train:** Invest in staff training on regulatory matters to foster a culture of compliance throughout your organization.

- **Record:** Maintain detailed records of all alcohol-related transactions to demonstrate compliance and facilitate audits.

Key areas of compliance to focus on include licensing, product registration, reporting, and marketing and advertising regulations. By prioritizing compliance in these areas, you can protect your business and build trust with regulators, partners, and customers.

2.6 Conclusion

Navigating the legal and regulatory landscape of the alcohol industry is not for the faint-hearted. It requires diligence, adaptability, and a commitment to continuous learning. However, as I've discovered throughout my career, the rewards of mastering this complex terrain are immense.

By understanding and complying with federal and state regulations, staying informed about legal changes, and prioritizing compliance, you can turn the legal landscape from a daunting obstacle into a powerful competitive advantage. You'll be better equipped to seize opportunities, avoid pitfalls, and build a thriving brand that stands the test of time.

As we move into the next chapter on developing effective brand strategies, remember that your knowledge of the legal and regulatory framework is a crucial foundation. By integrating your understanding of the rules with your strategic vision, you can create a brand that successfully navigates the three-tier system and resonates with your target audience, setting the stage for long-term growth and success in the market.

CHAPTER 3

Developing Your Brand Strategy

3.1 Introduction

Welcome to the world of brand strategy in the U.S. alcohol industry. In a market as crowded and competitive as ours, a strong brand strategy is not just a nice-to-have—it's an absolute necessity. Your brand is your promise to your customers, and every aspect of your strategy should reinforce that promise while aligning with the realities of the three-tier system.

In this chapter, we'll dive into the process of developing a compelling brand strategy that will help your product stand out on shelves, in bars, and in the minds of consumers. Drawing from my experience working with a diverse range of alcohol brands, from craft startups to established industry players, I'll guide you through the steps of creating a brand strategy that resonates with your target audience and sets you up for long-term success.

We'll start by defining your unique selling proposition (USP), the cornerstone of your brand identity. Then, we'll dive into the art and science of crafting a memorable brand story, designing eye-catching visual elements, and establishing a consistent brand voice. We'll explore the importance of understanding your target

13

market, conducting competitive analysis, and developing a channel strategy that leverages the strengths of the three-tier system.

Along the way, I'll share practical tips and real-world examples from my experience to help you navigate the challenges and seize the opportunities of building a strong alcohol brand. So, pour yourself a drink, and let's dive in!

3.2 Defining Your USP

Your USP is what sets your brand apart in a sea of competitors. It's the foundation upon which you'll build your entire brand strategy. To define your USP, start by identifying your brand's unique qualities. These could be your production methods, special ingredients, a unique heritage or story, or innovative product features.

Next, consider your target market. What do they value in an alcohol brand? What needs are currently unmet in the market and how does your product fulfill these needs? By understanding your target audience's preferences and pain points, you can craft a USP that speaks directly to them.

Finally, analyze your position in the competitive landscape. How can you offer something different from or better than existing brands? Is there a gap in the market that your brand can fill? A great example is Tito's Handmade Vodka, which successfully positioned itself as a high-quality, handcrafted vodka at a reasonable price point, filling a gap between premium and value vodkas.

3.3 Developing Your Brand Identity

Your brand identity is the face of your brand—it's how consumers perceive and connect with your product. A strong brand identity should encompass three key elements: your brand story, visual elements, and your brand voice.

Your brand story is the narrative that communicates your brand's origins, values, and mission. It should be authentic and compelling, and it should resonate with your target audience. When I worked with a family-owned winery, we spent a great deal of time crafting a story that highlighted the family's multigenerational dedication to winemaking and commitment to sustainability. This story became the backbone of their brand identity and helped them connect with consumers who valued tradition and environmental responsibility.

Visual elements, such as your logo, packaging design, and color scheme, are often the first point of contact with potential customers. In the alcohol industry, your bottle design and label play a crucial role in attracting attention on crowded shelves and conveying your brand's essence. Work with experienced designers to create a visual identity that is distinctive, memorable, and aligned with your brand story.

Your brand voice is the tone and personality you use in all your communications. It should be consistent across all platforms, from your website copy to your social media posts. Whether your brand voice is sophisticated, playful, rebellious, or traditional, ensure that it resonates with your target audience and accurately reflects your brand values.

3.4 Understanding Your Target Market

To create a brand strategy that truly connects with consumers, you need to have a deep understanding of your target market. Conduct thorough market research to develop detailed customer personas that include demographics, psychographics, and drinking habits. Identify the key market segments you want to target, whether it's millennials who value experiences and authenticity or connoisseurs who prioritize craftsmanship and heritage.

Understanding your target market's purchasing behaviors and preferences is also crucial. Where do they buy alcohol—in bars, retail stores, or online? What factors, such as price, recommendations, or reviews, influence their purchasing decisions? How do they typically consume your product category? By answering these questions, you can tailor your brand strategy and marketing efforts to effectively reach and engage your ideal customers.

3.5 Competitive Analysis

No brand exists in a vacuum. To develop a truly distinctive brand strategy, you need to have a thorough understanding of your competitive landscape. Start by identifying your direct and indirect competitors. Direct competitors are brands that offer similar products in your category, while indirect competitors are alternative beverages or experiences that compete for your target market's attention and dollars.

Analyze your competitors' strengths and weaknesses, from their product offerings and pricing to their brand positioning and marketing tactics. Look for gaps in the market that your brand can fill. Are there underserved segments or unmet needs that your competitors are overlooking? By identifying these opportunities, you can differentiate your brand and carve out a unique position in the market.

3.6 Channel Strategy

In the three-tier system, your channel strategy is just as important as your brand positioning. You need to determine where and how you'll sell your product, whether it's in bars and restaurants (on-premise sales), in retail stores (off-premise sales), or through e-commerce channels where legally permitted.

Each channel has its own unique requirements and opportunities. For example, on-premise sales may require building relationships with bar managers and developing cocktail recipes that showcase your product, while off-premise sales may involve securing prime shelf space and creating eye-catching point-of-sale (POS) displays.

Your channel strategy should also consider how to effectively leverage distributors, who play a crucial role in getting your product to market. Building strong relationships with distributors and understanding their priorities and challenges can help you get your brand in front of the right retailers and consumers.

3.7 Marketing and Promotion Strategies

With your brand identity, target market, competitive landscape, and channel strategy defined, it's time to develop a multifaceted marketing and promotion plan. In today's digital age, social media and online marketing are essential tools for reaching and engaging your target audience. Create compelling content that showcases your brand story and values, and use targeted advertising to get your message in front of the right people.

Event marketing and sponsorships are also powerful ways to build brand awareness and connect with consumers. Consider participating in industry events, such as wine and spirits festivals, or sponsoring local events that align with your brand identity. Partnering with influencers who authentically resonate with your brand can also help you reach new audiences and build credibility.

However, it's crucial to remember that alcohol marketing is heavily regulated. Always ensure that your promotional activities comply with federal and state laws, and be mindful of restrictions around social media advertising and influencer partnerships.

3.8 Measuring Brand Success

To continually refine and optimize your brand strategy, you need to measure your success against key performance indicators (KPIs). These may include brand awareness and recall, customer loyalty and repeat purchases, sales volume and market share, and social media engagement and sentiment.

Use a combination of surveys, social listening tools, sales data analysis, and web analytics to track these KPIs over time. Regularly review your performance and use these insights to make data-driven decisions about your brand strategy. If certain tactics aren't delivering the desired results, don't be afraid to pivot and try new approaches.

3.9 Adapting Your Strategy

The alcohol industry is constantly evolving, and your brand strategy needs to be adaptable to stay relevant and competitive. Keep a close eye on shifting consumer preferences and emerging trends, and be ready to innovate or adjust your product offerings accordingly. For example, the recent rise of hard seltzers and ready-to-drink cocktails has prompted many traditional beer and spirits brands to expand their portfolios to meet changing consumer demands.

Regulatory changes and new distribution opportunities can also require adjustments to your brand strategy. Stay informed about updates to federal and state laws that may impact your marketing or sales tactics, and be prepared to pivot your approach if necessary. The legalization of cannabis in some states, for instance, has created both challenges and opportunities for alcohol brands as they navigate this new competitive landscape.

As your brand grows and evolves, it's important to stay true to your core values and identity. Brands like Jack Daniel's have successfully adapted to changing times while maintaining their distinctive character and heritage. By consistently delivering on your brand promise and staying attuned to your target market's needs, you can build a loyal customer base that will support your brand for years to come.

3.10 Conclusion

Developing a strong brand strategy is both an art and a science. It requires creativity, market insight, adaptability, and a deep understanding of the unique challenges and opportunities of the three-tier system. By defining your USP, crafting a compelling brand identity, and tailoring your approach to your target market and competitive landscape, you can create a brand that stands out, resonates with consumers, and drives long-term success.

Remember, your brand strategy is not a one-and-done exercise; it's an ongoing process of refinement, adaptation, and growth. By staying attuned to your market, measuring your performance, and continually optimizing your approach, you can build a brand that not only survives but thrives in the dynamic and competitive world of the U.S. alcohol industry.

In the next chapter, we'll take a closer look at the first tier of the three-tier system and explore strategies for successfully navigating this critical stage of your brand's journey. From production and pricing to distribution and relationship-building, we'll cover everything you need to know to get your brand off to a strong start. So, let's move forward and continue our in-depth examination of the alcohol branding process and how to effectively navigate the three-tier system.

CHAPTER 4

Navigating the First Tier– Producers and Suppliers

4.1 Introduction

Welcome to the complex world of the first tier in the U.S. alcohol industry. In this chapter, we'll explore the pivotal role of producers and suppliers, the craftsmen and visionaries who create the products that eventually find their way to consumers' glasses. Whether you're a small craft brewer with dreams of national distribution or an established winery seeking to expand your market share, understanding the dynamics of the first tier is essential to your success.

As someone who has worked closely with producers of all sizes, from family-owned vineyards to large-scale operations, I can attest to the unique challenges and opportunities that exist within this tier. Navigating the complex regulatory landscape, building strong distributor relationships, and crafting a compelling brand identity are just a few of the key elements that producers must master to thrive in the three-tier system.

In this chapter, we'll dive into the diverse landscape of producers, explore the licensing and regulatory considerations they face, and discuss strategies for effectively interacting with distributors.

By the end of this chapter, you'll have a deeper understanding of the first tier and be better equipped to make informed decisions as you navigate the complexities of alcohol distribution in the United States.

4.2 Types of Producer in the Alcohol Industry

The first tier of the alcohol industry comprises a wide range of producers, each with its own unique characteristics and challenges. Let's take a closer look at the main types of producer:

- **Wineries:** From small family-owned vineyards to large-scale operations, wineries are the backbone of the U.S. wine industry. As of 2021, there were over 11,000 wineries in the country, with California leading the way with about 4,700 wineries. Having worked with numerous wineries throughout my career, I've seen firsthand the passion and craftsmanship that goes into every bottle of wine.

- **Distilleries:** These producers create the spirits that many of us enjoy, from vodka and whiskey to gin and rum. The craft distilling scene has experienced explosive growth in recent years, with 2,290 active craft distillers. The rise of craft distilleries has brought new levels of innovation and variety to the spirits category.

- **Breweries:** From microbreweries to major national brands, breweries are responsible for producing the beers that millions of Americans enjoy. In 2021, there were over 9,000 breweries in the U.S., with craft brewers accounting for about 12 percent of the beer market by volume. The craft beer revolution has reshaped the brewing landscape, offering consumers an unprecedented array of styles and flavors.

- **Importers:** These entities bring foreign-produced alcoholic beverages into the U.S. market, introducing international brands to American consumers. Importers play a crucial role in expanding the diversity of products available and catering to the growing demand for global flavors and experiences.

- **Brand Owners:** These companies may contract out production but own and market the brand, allowing for flexibility and often a lower initial capital investment. Brand owners focus on building strong brand identities and connecting with consumers, while leaving the production to specialized facilities.

Each type of producer faces unique challenges and opportunities within the three-tier system. A small craft distillery might struggle to gain the attention of large distributors but could leverage its local roots for DTC sales where allowed. On the other hand, a major national brand might have strong distributor relationships but need to work hard to maintain relevance in a market increasingly drawn to craft and local products.

Understanding the nuances of each producer type is essential for developing effective strategies and building successful relationships within the three-tier system.

4.3 Licensing and Regulatory Considerations for Producers

One of the most complex aspects of being a producer in the U.S. alcohol industry is navigating the intricate web of federal and state regulations. Each jurisdiction has its own set of requirements, making compliance a constant challenge. As someone who has helped numerous producers navigate this regulatory maze, I can't stress enough the importance of staying informed and seeking expert guidance when needed.

Key regulatory considerations for producers include:

- **Federal Licensing:** All producers must obtain a Federal Basic Permit from the TTB. This permit is the foundation of your operation and is required before you can begin producing or selling alcohol.

- **State Licensing:** Requirements vary widely by state and may include production licenses, wholesaler licenses, and direct shipping permits. It's crucial to research the specific requirements in each state where you plan to operate and ensure that you have all the necessary licenses and permits in place.

- **Labeling and Formula Approval:** All alcoholic beverage labels must be approved by the TTB, and some products, such as flavored malt beverages or certain spirits, require formula approval. Ensuring that your labels and formulas meet all regulatory requirements is essential to avoid costly delays and compliance issues.

- **Compliance Obligations:** Producers must regularly file production and sales reports, pay taxes, and adhere to advertising regulations. Developing a robust compliance program and staying on top of these obligations is critical to maintaining good standing with regulatory agencies.

It's important to remember that regulations can vary significantly by product type and state. A brewery in Colorado will face different regulatory challenges from a distillery in Kentucky or a winery in New York. Always consult with legal experts who specialize in alcohol regulation to ensure that you're meeting all applicable requirements.

In my experience, investing in a strong compliance foundation from the outset can save you countless headaches down the road. By staying informed, seeking expert advice, and building compliance into your operations, you'll be better positioned to navigate the regulatory landscape and focus on what you do best – creating exceptional products.

4.4 Interacting with Distributors

In the three-tier system, your relationship with distributors is one of the most critical factors in your success. Distributors are your gateway to the market, and building strong, mutually beneficial relationships with them is essential. As someone who has worked on both sides of the producer–distributor relationship, I've learned that a strategic approach and ongoing effort are key to making these partnerships work.

Here are some strategies for effectively interacting with distributors:

- **Communicate Regularly:** Keep your distributors informed about your products, your brand, and your plans. Provide comprehensive product information and training to help them understand and effectively sell your offerings. Regular check-ins, whether in person, by phone, or via email, can help keep your brand top-of-mind and address any issues that may arise.

- **Negotiate Agreements:** When setting up distribution agreements, consider factors like territory, portfolio representation, and performance metrics. Be clear about your expectations and what you're offering in return. Remember, a good distribution agreement is one that benefits both parties and sets the stage for a long-term, successful relationship.

- **Stand Out:** In a crowded market, it's crucial to differentiate your brand and make it easy for distributors to understand and sell your products. Develop a clear, compelling brand story and be prepared to demonstrate your market potential, especially if you're a smaller producer. Providing strong marketing support, attractive packaging, and USPs can help your brand stand out in a distributor's portfolio.

- **Give Ongoing Support:** Your work doesn't end once your product is in distribution. Provide high-quality marketing materials, participate in sales meetings and ride-alongs, and consider offering incentives for meeting sales targets. Be a partner to your distributor, and work together to grow your brand and achieve mutual success.

Above all, remember that your success and your distributor's success are intertwined. Approach the relationship with respect, understanding, and a willingness to collaborate. By building strong, supportive relationships with your distributors, you'll be better positioned to navigate the challenges of the three-tier system and achieve long-term success in the market.

4.5 Conclusion

Navigating the first tier of the U.S. alcohol industry as a producer requires a multifaceted approach. Success in this complex landscape involves understanding and complying with intricate regulations, building strong relationships with distributors and retailers, crafting a compelling brand identity, and staying adaptable in a rapidly evolving industry.

As we've explored in this chapter, each type of producer—from wineries and distilleries to breweries and importers—faces unique challenges and opportunities within the three-tier system. By understanding the nuances of your specific industry segment and developing strategies tailored to your goals, you can effectively navigate the first tier and set the foundation for success throughout the entire three-tier system.

Remember, your role as a producer extends far beyond creating a quality product. You are the origin point of the three-tier system, and your decisions and actions have a ripple effect throughout the entire distribution chain. By mastering the elements we've discussed in this chapter—regulatory compliance, distributor relationships, brand-building, and adaptability—you'll be well-equipped to thrive in the complex and challenging world of alcohol production and distribution.

As we move forward into the next chapter, we'll explore the second tier of the system—distribution—and delve into the strategies and considerations that can help you maximize your success in this critical phase of your product's journey to the consumer. Until then, keep crafting, keep innovating, and keep navigating the competitive landscape of alcohol production and distribution.

CHAPTER 5

Mastering the Second Tier–Distribution

5.1 Introduction

Welcome to the heart of the three-tier system: the distribution tier. In the complex world of U.S. alcohol sales, distributors are not just a link between producers and retailers; they are the vital backbone of the industry. As someone who has worked as both a distributor and a supplier, I can attest to the critical role this middle tier plays in the success of any alcohol brand.

Distributors are more than just logistics providers; they are brand ambassadors, market experts, and often the key to unlocking new opportunities for growth. Understanding and effectively partnering with distributors can mean the difference between a brand that thrives and one that struggles to gain traction.

In this chapter, we'll dive deep into the world of distribution, exploring the landscape and offering insights into selecting the right partners, negotiating favorable terms, and building successful relationships. I'll share my experiences and strategies from both sides of the distributor–supplier relationship to help you navigate this critical tier and set your brand up for long-term success.

tanding the Distributor Landscape

n landscape has undergone significant changes in ̶r̶e̶c̶e̶n̶t̶ ̶y̶e̶a̶r̶s̶, shaped by market forces, regulatory shifts, and industry consolidation. As of 2021, the top 10 distributors control over 80 percent of the market share, while the total number of distributors has decreased from about 3,000 in the 1990s to fewer than 1,000 today.

Within this evolving landscape, distributors can be categorized into three main types:

- **National Distributors:** These large-scale operators have extensive reach across multiple states, offering broad coverage and significant resources.

- **Regional Distributors:** Focused on specific geographic areas, these distributors often provide more personalized service and have deep knowledge of their local markets.

- **Specialized Distributors:** These distributors concentrate on specific categories, such as craft beer or fine wine, and offer expertise and targeted market access within their niche.

Technology is also playing an increasingly important role in distribution. Many distributors now offer online ordering platforms, real-time inventory tracking, and data analytics tools to help suppliers make informed decisions and optimize their sales strategies.

Understanding the nuances of the distributor landscape is crucial for developing an effective distribution strategy. By knowing the strengths and limitations of each type of distributor, you

can make informed choices about which partners are best suited .
help you achieve your brand's goals.

5.3 Selecting the Right Distributor

Choosing the right distribution partner is one of the most important decisions you'll make as a supplier. It's about not just who can move your product but who can effectively grow your brand. When evaluating potential distributors, consider the following criteria:

- **Market Coverage and Penetration:** Look beyond simple geography and assess their relationships with key accounts in your target market. A distributor with strong connections and a proven track record in your desired outlets can be invaluable.

- **Sales Force Size and Expertise:** Evaluate both the quantity and the quality of their sales team. A knowledgeable, well-trained, and motivated sales force can make a significant impact on your brand's success.

- **Portfolio Fit:** Ensure that your brand complements rather than competes with the distributor's existing portfolio. You want your brand to stand out and receive the attention it deserves.

- **Technological Capabilities:** Assess their use of modern tools for ordering, inventory management, and data analysis. A technologically advanced distributor can provide valuable insights and efficiencies.

For smaller brands, standing out in a crowded market and attracting the attention of distributors can be challenging. However,

pelling brand story that resonates with your target
be a powerful tool. It's not just about demonstrating
:ntial through consumer research or successful test
.... lts; you need to craft a narrative that captivates and
engages your audience.

In my experience, the most successful supplier–distributor
partnerships are built on a foundation of shared values, mutual
respect, and a genuine belief in the brand's potential. Take the time
to find a distributor who not only has the capabilities you need but
also shares your vision and passion for your brand.

5.4 Negotiating Contracts and Terms

Once you've identified the right distribution partner, it's time to
negotiate the terms of your agreement. This is a critical step that
can have long-lasting implications for your brand's success, so it's
important to approach it with care and diligence.

Key elements to consider when negotiating distribution
agreements include:

- **Territory Definitions:** Clearly outline the geographic
  areas in which the distributor will have the right to sell
  your products.

- **Performance Expectations:** Set clear targets for sales volume, market share, and other key metrics, and establish
  regular review periods to assess performance.

- **Marketing Support Commitments:** Specify the level
  of marketing support you expect from the distributor,
  including promotional activities, sampling events, and
  sales incentives.

- **Termination Clauses:** Pay close attention to the conditions under which either party can terminate the agreement, and ensure that they align with your long-term goals and state-specific franchise laws.

Speaking of state franchise laws, it's crucial to be mindful of these regulations when negotiating agreements. These laws can significantly impact your ability to terminate or change distributors, so it's essential to understand their implications in each state where you operate.

Always consult with legal experts who specialize in alcohol distribution when drafting and negotiating agreements. These professionals can help you navigate the complexities of state-specific regulations and ensure that your contracts protect your interests while fostering strong, mutually beneficial partnerships.

5.5 Building Strong Distributor Relationships

Success in the distribution tier hinges on building strong, collaborative relationships with your distribution partners. As someone who has worked on both sides of this equation, I can't stress enough the importance of open communication, transparency, and mutual support.

Here are some key strategies for fostering successful distributor relationships:

- **Regular Communication:** Schedule monthly or quarterly reviews to discuss performance, challenges, and opportunities. Consistent, open dialogue helps maintain alignment and address issues before they become problems.

- **Transparency:** Be transparent about your production capabilities, marketing plans, and any challenges you're facing. A distributor who understands your business can be a valuable partner in finding solutions and driving growth.

- **Product Training:** Provide comprehensive information about your products, including production methods, tasting notes, and brand stories. A well-informed sales team is better equipped to effectively represent your brand in the market.

- **Sales Support:** Participate in ride-alongs with distributor sales reps and attend key account meetings. Your presence and expertise can make a significant impact on sales efforts and demonstrate your commitment to the partnership.

Brand representatives play a crucial role in managing distributor relationships. They serve as the face of your brand, ensuring consistent communication and support. Key responsibilities include conducting regular market visits, providing sales and marketing support, and acting as a liaison between the supplier and distributor teams.

Building strong distributor relationships takes time, effort, and a genuine commitment to mutual success. By approaching these partnerships with respect, transparency, and a willingness to collaborate, you can create a solid foundation for your brand's growth and long-term success in the market.

5.6 Pricing Strategies in Distribution

Effective pricing is critical to your success in the three-tier system, and it requires careful consideration of margins at each tier. One key decision is whether to use an FOB (freight on board) or delivered pricing model.

Under FOB pricing, the distributor takes ownership of the product at your facility and is responsible for the cost of shipping to their warehouse. This gives you less control over the final price to retailers, as the distributor will add their margin and any shipping costs.

With delivered pricing, you retain ownership of the product until it reaches the distributor's warehouse and are responsible for the shipping costs. This allows you to maintain greater control over the final price, but it also means you'll need to factor shipping costs into your margins.

Be aware of typical distributor margins in your category. For wine and spirits, distributor margins typically range from 25 percent to 30 percent, while beer distributor margins are usually between 25 percent and 35 percent. Understanding these margins can help you set realistic pricing strategies that allow for profitability at each tier.

In some states, price posting laws require suppliers to file their prices publicly. These laws can limit your flexibility in pricing and promotions, so it's crucial to understand the regulations in each market you enter. Building a strong working knowledge of state-specific pricing regulations will help you avoid costly mistakes and maximize your brand's profitability.

d Support and Marketing through tion

Your distributor relationships can be a powerful amplifier for your brand support and marketing efforts. By collaborating effectively with your distribution partners, you can extend your reach, gain valuable market insights, and drive sales growth.

Consider these strategies for maximizing your brand support and marketing through distribution:

- **Joint Marketing Plans:** Develop marketing plans in collaboration with your distributor, aligning your brand goals with their capabilities and resources. A coordinated approach can help you achieve greater impact and efficiency.

- **Co-op Advertising Programs:** Many distributors offer co-op advertising programs that can help extend your marketing reach. By partnering with your distributor on these programs, you can share costs and gain access to additional promotional opportunities.

- **Sales Team Training:** Provide your distributor's sales team with comprehensive training materials, including product knowledge, brand stories, and sales techniques. A well-trained sales force is your most valuable asset in the market.

- **Performance Incentives:** Offer sales incentives tied to specific performance metrics to motivate distributor sales teams. Whether it's through contests, bonuses, or other rewards, aligning incentives with your brand goals can help drive focus and results.

By working closely with your distribution partners on brand support and marketing initiatives, you can leverage their resources, relationships, and market expertise to drive sales, build brand awareness, and achieve your growth objectives.

5.8 Navigating Challenges in Distribution

Even the most successful supplier–distributor relationships can face challenges. Some common issues include inventory management, underperformance, and managing multi-state distribution. Proactively addressing these challenges is key to maintaining a healthy, productive partnership.

To avoid out-of-stocks and overstocks, implement robust inventory tracking systems that provide real-time visibility in your supply chain. Work closely with your distributor to forecast demand, monitor inventory levels, and adjust production as needed.

If you encounter underperformance from a distributor, address it promptly through open, honest communication. Collaborate with your distribution partner to identify the root causes of the issue and develop a clear plan for improvement. Set specific, measurable goals and monitor progress regularly.

For suppliers with multi-state distribution, managing relationships across different markets can be complex. Consider implementing a regional management structure to provide localized support and expertise. This approach allows you to navigate the nuances of each market while maintaining a cohesive overall strategy.

In my experience, the key to overcoming challenges in distribution is to approach them as opportunities for collaboration and growth. By working closely with your distribution partners, maintaining open lines of communication, and staying focused on your shared goals, you can navigate even the toughest obstacles and emerge stronger.

5.9 The Future of Distribution in the Three-Tier System

As the alcohol industry continues to evolve, so too will the role of distributors in the three-tier system. Emerging trends and technologies are reshaping the landscape, presenting both challenges and opportunities for suppliers and distributors alike.

One significant trend is the growing importance of e-commerce and DTC sales. While these channels are still limited by regulations in many states, the COVID-19 pandemic has accelerated the shift toward online purchasing and home delivery. As these channels continue to grow, distributors will need to adapt and find ways to integrate them into their business models.

Another trend is the increasing focus on data analytics and digital tools. Distributors who can leverage data to gain insights into consumer behavior, market trends, and sales performance will be better positioned to serve their supplier partners and drive growth. Suppliers who can access and utilize this data will be able to make more informed decisions about product development, pricing, and marketing strategies.

As the industry evolves, the role of distributors in the three-tier system will likely continue to expand beyond the traditional functions of logistics and sales. Successful distributors will be those who can adapt to changing market conditions, leverage new technologies, and provide value-added services to their supplier partners.

For suppliers, staying attuned to these trends and partnering with forward-thinking distributors will be key to navigating the future of the three-tier system. By embracing innovation, collaboration, and adaptability, suppliers and distributors can work together to overcome challenges and seize new opportunities in the ever-changing alcohol industry.

5.10 Keys to Success in the Distribution Tier

Throughout this chapter, we've explored the many facets of mastering the distribution tier, from understanding the landscape and selecting the right partners to building strong relationships and navigating challenges. As we conclude, I want to leave you with some key takeaways that can help you unlock success in this critical tier.

- **Choose Your Partners Wisely:** The right distributor can be the key to unlocking your brand's full potential. Look for partners who share your values, vision, and commitment to success.

- **Build Relationships Based on Trust and Transparency:** Open, honest communication is the foundation of any successful distributor partnership. Be transparent about your goals, challenges, and expectations, and work collaboratively to achieve shared success.

- **Invest in Supporting Your Distributor's Efforts:** Your success is intertwined with your distributor's success. Provide the tools, resources, and support they need to effectively represent your brand in the market.

- **Stay Agile and Adaptable:** The alcohol industry is constantly evolving, and success in the distribution tier requires the ability to adapt to changing conditions. Stay attuned to market trends, regulatory shifts, and new opportunities, and be ready to pivot when necessary.

- **Never Stop Learning and Improving:** The most successful suppliers are those who are constantly seeking to learn, grow, and improve. Stay curious, seek out new insights and best practices, and be willing to try new approaches.

Mastering the distribution tier is a journey, not a destination. It requires ongoing effort, collaboration, and a commitment to excellence. But, for those who are willing to put in the work, the rewards can be significant.

As you navigate the complexities of the distribution tier, remember that you're not alone. Your distribution partners are there to support you, and there's a wealth of knowledge and experience in the industry to draw upon. By staying focused on your goals, building strong relationships, and embracing the challenges and opportunities of the three-tier system, you can achieve long-term success and growth for your brand.

CHAPTER 6

Conquering the Third Tier—Retail

6.1 Introduction

Welcome to the critical and complex world of the third tier—retail. This is where your brand comes face-to-face with consumers, and where the success of your hard work in production and distribution is ultimately put to the test. The retail tier is a complex, dynamic landscape that requires a strategic approach and a deep understanding of both on-premise and off-premise channels.

As someone who has led sales teams targeting both chain and independent retailers, I can attest to the critical importance of mastering this tier. Whether you're a small craft producer or a large national brand, your success in the retail tier will largely determine your overall success in the alcohol industry.

In this chapter, we'll explore the intricacies of navigating the retail landscape. We'll dive into the unique characteristics and challenges of on-premise and off-premise channels, discuss strategies for building strong relationships with retailers, and share insights on how to overcome common obstacles. By the end of this chapter, you'll have a comprehensive toolkit for conquering the third tier and driving long-term growth for your brand.

So, let's step into the fast-paced, ever-changing world of alcohol retail and discover the strategies and tactics that will help you succeed in this critical tier.

6.2 Understanding the Retail Landscape

The retail tier in the alcohol industry is a diverse and complex ecosystem, encompassing a wide range of businesses with varying needs, priorities, and challenges. To develop an effective retail strategy, it's essential to understand the unique characteristics of each type of retail outlet.

On-premise establishments, such as bars, restaurants, hotels, and event venues, are where consumers enjoy your products in a social setting. These outlets offer the opportunity to create memorable experiences, build brand loyalty, and generate word-of-mouth buzz. However, they also require a tailored approach that takes into account factors such as menu placement, staff training, and event activation.

Off-premise retailers, including supermarkets, liquor stores, convenience stores, and online shops, are where consumers purchase your products for consumption at home. These outlets often drive higher sales volumes and provide a more stable revenue stream. Success in the off-premise channel requires a focus on shelf placement, promotional strategies, and category management.

Understanding the nuances of each retail channel is crucial for developing a targeted, effective sales and marketing strategy. By tailoring your approach to the specific needs and challenges of each type of outlet, you can maximize your brand's impact and drive long-term growth in the retail tier.

6.3 On-Premise Strategies

On-premise sales can be a powerful driver of brand awareness, consumer loyalty, and overall success in the alcohol industry. Here are three key strategies for excelling in the on-premise channel:

- **Menu Placement:** Securing a coveted spot on a restaurant's or bar's menu can significantly boost your brand's visibility and sales. During my time as a distributor, we found that getting a wine placed by-the-glass could triple or quadruple its sales volume in that account. To achieve optimal menu placement, work closely with the establishment's beverage director or sommelier to showcase how your product complements their menu concept. Offer staff training to ensure that your product is properly presented and recommended to customers and consider creating custom cocktails or food pairings that highlight your product's unique qualities.

- **Brand Activation Events:** Hosting events at on-premise locations can create memorable experiences that drive long-term brand loyalty. Organize tastings, meet-the-maker events, or themed parties that align with your brand's identity and values. Partner with the venue to create special promotions or limited-time offerings that encourage trial and repeat purchases. Use these events as opportunities to gather valuable consumer feedback and build relationships with key account staff.

- **Staff Education:** Well-informed staff can be your best brand ambassadors in the on-premise channel. Invest time and resources in educating bartenders, servers, and other on-premise staff about your products. Develop comprehensive training materials that cover your brand story, production methods, and serving suggestions. Organize regular training sessions or ride-alongs with your sales team to keep your brand top-of-mind and ensure that staff are equipped to recommend your products with confidence. Consider implementing incentive programs that reward staff for successfully promoting your products and driving sales.

By implementing these strategies, you can build a strong presence in the on-premise channel, create meaningful connections with consumers, and drive long-term brand loyalty and success.

6.4 Off-Premise Strategies

While on-premise sales are crucial for building brand awareness and loyalty, off-premise sales are often the backbone of an alcohol brand's revenue stream. Here are three key strategies for succeeding in the off-premise channel:

- **Shelf Placement and Merchandising:** In the crowded off-premise retail environment, your product's location and visibility can make or break its success. During my time at Epic Wines & Spirits, we saw that moving our brands to eye-level shelves could increase sales by up to 30 percent. To optimize your shelf placement, negotiate for prime positions, endcap displays, or featured placements that maximize your brand's visibility. Design eye-catching packaging and POS materials that stand out on crowded shelves and communicate your brand's unique value proposition. Regularly audit your placements to ensure compliance with agreements and optimal visibility.

- **Promotions and Pricing:** Strategic promotions can be a powerful tool for driving trial, repeat purchases, and overall sales volume in the off-premise channel. Develop a mix of promotional activities, including temporary price reductions, multi-buy offers, and bundle deals, that incentivize consumers to try your product and stock up for future consumption. Time your promotions to align with seasonal trends, holidays, or local events that are likely to drive increased demand. However, be cautious of over-promoting, which can erode your brand's perceived value and train consumers to only purchase your products when they are on discount.

- **Category Management:** Positioning your brand as a category leader can lead to preferential treatment from off-premise retailers and a larger share of the overall market. Provide retailers with data-driven insights about category trends, consumer preferences, and growth op-portunities. Propose planograms or category resets that optimize the overall shopping experience and benefit both your brand and the retailer's bottom line. For larger accounts, consider offering category captaincy services that leverage your expertise to drive mutual growth and strengthen your partnership with key retailers.

By implementing these strategies, you can build a strong, profitable presence in the off-premise channel and ensure that your brand is well-positioned for long-term success in the retail tier.

6.5 Building Relationships with Retailers

Strong relationships with retailers are the foundation of success in the third tier. Here are four key strategies for building and maintaining these crucial partnerships:

- **Understand Their Business:** Take the time to learn about each retailer's unique business model, challenges, and goals. Regularly review their sales data and market performance to identify opportunities for growth and improvement. Stay informed about their company news, expansion plans, and changes in leadership, and use this knowledge to tailor your proposals and recommendations to their specific needs and objectives.

- **Provide Value beyond Your Product:** Position yourself as a valuable partner, not just another vendor. Offer market insights, consumer trends, and competitive intelligence that helps retailers stay ahead of the curve. Be proactive in helping them solve problems, even if they aren't directly related to your products. Serve as a trusted resource for industry news, regulatory updates, and best practices that can help them navigate the complex alcohol retail landscape.

- **Communicate Consistently:** Maintain open and regular lines of communication with your retail partners. Schedule regular business reviews to discuss performance, challenges, and opportunities, and be proactive in addressing any issues or concerns. Be responsive to their inquiries and feedback, even outside of normal business hours. Use a mix of communication channels, including in-person visits, phone calls, and digital platforms, to stay connected and build strong, personal relationships.

- **Deliver on Promises:** Reliability and follow-through are essential for building trust and credibility with retailers. Ensure timely delivery of products and promotional materials, and honor all commitments, whether they relate to pricing agreements, marketing support, or product exclusivity. If issues or delays arise, be transparent and proactive in communicating with retailers and working to find mutually beneficial solutions.

By investing in these relationship-building strategies, you can establish your brand as a trusted, valuable partner for retailers and lay the foundation for long-term success in the third tier.

6.6 Navigating Challenges in the Retail Tier

While the retail tier offers tremendous opportunities for brand growth and success, it also presents a unique set of challenges that require careful navigation. Here are three common challenges and strategies for overcoming them:

- **Managing Inventory:** Balancing stock levels to avoid both out-of-stocks and overstocks is crucial for maintaining strong relationships with retailers and ensuring consistent product availability for consumers. Implement data analytics tools and processes to accurately predict demand and optimize inventory levels across different retail channels and accounts. Where possible, work with retailers to implement just-in-time delivery systems that minimize inventory holding costs and reduce the risk of spoilage or expiration. Develop clear policies and procedures for handling slow-moving inventory or seasonal products, and work proactively with retailers to find creative solutions for minimizing waste and maximizing profitability.

- **Dealing with Consolidation:** The ongoing trend toward retail consolidation can make it challenging for smaller brands to gain traction and secure prime shelf space in larger chain accounts. To overcome this challenge, focus on building strong relationships with key decision-makers in large retail organizations and be prepared to demonstrate the unique value and growth potential of your brand. Consider partnering with other complementary brands to offer a more compelling, diversified portfolio to large retailers, and explore opportunities for cross-promotional activities or shared marketing initiatives. At the same time, don't neglect the importance of independent retailers, who often provide opportunities for higher margins, greater flexibility, and more targeted brand-building efforts.

- **Adapting to E-commerce:** The rapid growth of online alcohol sales presents both opportunities and challenges for brands navigating the retail tier. To succeed in the e-commerce channel, ensure that your products are well-represented on retailers' online platforms, with compelling descriptions, high-quality images, and accurate product information. Consider developing e-commerce-specific packaging or bundle offers that are optimized for online sales and delivery. Stay informed about evolving regulations around online alcohol sales in different states, and work closely with retailers to ensure compliance with all applicable laws and guidelines.

By proactively addressing these challenges and adapting your strategies to the changing retail landscape, you can position your brand for success and build a strong, resilient presence in the third tier.

6.7 Conclusion

Conquering the retail tier is a critical component of long-term success in the alcohol industry. By understanding the unique characteristics and challenges of on-premise and off-premise channels, developing targeted strategies for each, and building strong relationships with retailers, you can drive brand awareness, consumer loyalty, and profitable growth.

As you navigate the complex and ever-changing retail landscape, remember to stay agile, adaptable, and focused on delivering value to both your retail partners and your end consumers. By consistently providing high-quality products, exceptional service, and data-driven insights, you can establish your brand as a leader in the retail tier and lay the foundation for long-term success in the alcohol industry.

CHAPTER 7

Marketing within the Three-Tier System

7.1 Introduction

Welcome to the intricate and regulated world of marketing within the three-tier system. As we've explored throughout this book, the alcohol industry is governed by a unique set of regulations that significantly impact how brands can promote their products. Navigating this landscape requires a balance of creativity, strategic planning, and a good understanding of the legal framework.

In this chapter, we'll explore the strategic and tactical aspects of marketing within the three-tier system. We'll explore the unique challenges and opportunities that exist within this regulated environment and provide you with practical strategies for building a strong, resonant brand presence. From understanding the regulatory landscape and developing compliant brand activation strategies, to leveraging distributor resources and crafting integrated marketing campaigns, we'll cover all the essential elements of effective alcohol marketing.

As someone who has worked on both the supplier and the distributor sides of the business, I've seen firsthand the importance of smart, strategic marketing in driving brand success. Whether you're a small craft producer or a large multinational brand, the principles and tactics we'll discuss in this chapter will help you navigate the complexities of the three-tier system and build a strong, lasting brand.

So, let's focus on the critical aspects of alcohol marketing and explore the strategies and insights that will help you succeed in this challenging industry.

7.2 Understanding the Regulatory Landscape

Before we delve into specific marketing strategies, it's essential to understand the regulatory environment that shapes alcohol marketing. Central to this framework are the "tied house" laws, which aim to maintain the independence of each tier and prevent vertical integration.

Tied house laws significantly impact marketing activities by:

- **Prohibiting Inducements:** Producers and distributors are generally not allowed to provide items of value to retailers to influence their purchasing decisions. This restriction applies to certain promotional items, equipment, and excessive entertainment.

- **Limiting Cross-Tier Ownership:** In most cases, a company cannot have ownership interests across different tiers, which affects marketing partnerships and collaborations.

- **Restricting Advertising Support:** There are often strict rules about how producers and distributors can support or be involved in retailer advertising.

- **Impacting Promotional Activities:** Many common marketing tactics in other industries, such as paying for preferred shelf space or funding retailer-specific advertising, may be prohibited or strictly limited.

In addition to tied house laws, alcohol marketing is subject to federal regulations enforced by the TTB. These regulations prohibit false or misleading statements, require mandatory disclosure of alcohol content, and restrict health claims.

Each state also has its own set of rules governing alcohol marketing, which can vary widely. Some states restrict or prohibit certain types of promotion, like happy hours or two-for-one specials, while others may have limitations on where and how alcohol can be advertised.

Finally, many industry associations have their own codes of conduct for responsible marketing. Adhering to these guidelines can help maintain positive relationships with regulators and the public.

Understanding and navigating this complex regulatory landscape is crucial for developing compliant and effective marketing strategies within the three-tier system.

7.3 Brand Activation Strategies

Brand activation strategies are designed to create meaningful, memorable experiences that connect consumers with your brand. When developing these strategies within the three-tier system, it's essential to ensure that all activities comply with tied house laws and other relevant regulations.

Here are some compliant and effective brand activation strategies:

- **Experiential Marketing:** Create immersive experiences that allow consumers to interact with your brand in a memorable way. This could include hosting tasting events or cocktail classes featuring your products, sponsoring local events that align with your brand values, or creating pop-up experiences that showcase your brand story. During my time at Schug Winery, we found great success with vineyard tours that allowed visitors to see the winemaking process firsthand, creating a lasting connection to our brand.

- **Digital Engagement:** Leverage digital platforms to reach and engage with your target audience. Develop a strong social media presence with consistent, engaging content that resonates with your brand identity. Use targeted digital advertising to reach specific consumer segments based on their interests, behaviors, and demographics. Create virtual experiences, such as online tastings or behind-the-scenes videos, to connect with consumers in a more intimate, interactive way.

- **Collaborations and Partnerships:** Partner with complementary brands or influencers to expand your reach and tap into new audiences. This could involve collaborating with local chefs on food pairings that showcase your products, partnering with non-alcohol brands that share your target audience and values, or working with influencers who authentically align with your brand identity. The key is to find partnerships that create value for all parties involved and amplify your brand message in a credible, authentic way.

- **Limited Releases and Special Editions:** Create buzz and drive demand by offering exclusive, limited-edition products. This could include seasonal releases that tap into current trends or consumer preferences, retailer-exclusive offerings that strengthen key partnerships, or special packaging and collaborations that generate excitement and collectibility. The scarcity and uniqueness of these offerings can help drive trial, build loyalty, and generate word-of-mouth buzz for your brand.

By implementing these brand activation strategies in a way that is both creative and compliant, you can create powerful, lasting connections with consumers that drive brand awareness, preference, and loyalty.

7.4 Leveraging Distributor Resources

Your distributors are not just logistics providers; they are valuable partners in your marketing efforts. By leveraging their resources and expertise, you can amplify your brand message, reach new audiences, and drive sales growth.

Here's how to make the most of your distributor partnerships:

- **Co-op Marketing Programs:** Many distributors offer co-op marketing funds to support brand-building activities. These funds can be used for a wide range of initiatives, from traditional print and digital advertising to experiential marketing and event sponsorships. To maximize the impact of these funds, develop joint marketing plans that align with both your brand goals and the distributor's objectives. Propose innovative uses of co-op funds that go beyond traditional tactics and track the return on investment (ROI) of these initiatives to justify continued investment.

- **Distributor Sales Team Education:** Your distributor's sales team is your front line in the market, interacting with retailers and influencing purchasing decisions. By investing in comprehensive training and education for these teams, you can turn them into powerful brand ambassadors. Develop training materials that cover your brand story, production methods, key selling points, and target consumer profiles. Conduct regular training sessions, both in person and virtually, to keep your brand top-of-mind and ensure that sales reps are equipped to effectively promote your products.

- **Data and Market Insights:** Distributors have access to valuable data on sales trends, consumer behaviors, and market dynamics. By leveraging these insights, you can make more informed decisions about product development, pricing, promotions, and distribution strategies. Request regular reports from your distributor partners and use this data to identify opportunities for growth, optimize your marketing efforts, and stay ahead of the competition.

- **Event Support:** Distributors often have strong relationships with key accounts and can provide valuable support for brand activation events. Partner with your distributors on trade shows, industry events, and consumer tastings to maximize your reach and impact. Leverage your distributor's connections to secure prime placements at local festivals, tastings, and other high-profile events. Collaborate on retailer events, using the distributor's relationships to drive participation and ensure a successful outcome.

By leveraging your distributor's resources and expertise, you can extend your marketing reach, gain valuable insights, and build strong relationships across all three tiers of the system.

7.5 Integrated Marketing Campaigns

The most effective marketing campaigns in the three-tier system are those that seamlessly integrate activities across all tiers, creating a cohesive, powerful brand experience for consumers. By coordinating efforts among producers, distributors, and retailers, you can maximize the impact of your marketing spend and drive better results.

Here's an example of how an integrated marketing campaign might work:

Campaign: Summer Cocktail Launch

- **Tier 1 (Producer):** Develop a new summer-themed cocktail recipe featuring your product. Create digital content, including videos and social media posts, showcasing the cocktail and its unique flavor profile. Develop POS materials and tasting notes to support on-premise and off-premise activation.

- **Tier 2 (Distributor):** Train the distributor sales team on the new cocktail, its key selling points, and your target accounts. Use co-op funds to create additional POS materials, such as table tents, menu inserts, and shelf talkers. Work with the distributor to identify key accounts for launch events and promotions.

- **Tier 3 (Retail):** Partner with key on-premise accounts to feature the cocktail on their menus and host tasting events to drive trial. Work with off-premise retailers to secure prime shelf placement and feature the cocktail in their summer promotions. Use social media and digital advertising to drive consumers to participating accounts and generate buzz around the launch.

By coordinating efforts across all three tiers, you can create a cohesive, impactful campaign that drives trial, builds brand awareness, and generates sales momentum. The key is to ensure that each tier's activities are aligned with the overall campaign goals and that there is clear communication and collaboration throughout the process.

7.6 Measuring Marketing Effectiveness

In the complex world of three-tier marketing, it's essential to measure the effectiveness of your efforts to optimize your spend and demonstrate ROI to stakeholders. By tracking key metrics and using data to inform your decisions, you can continually refine your marketing strategies and allocate resources more effectively.

Here are some key metrics to track:

- **Sales Lift:** Monitor sales performance during and after marketing campaigns to assess their impact on revenue growth. Compare sales data to prior periods and control markets to isolate the effect of your marketing activities.

- **Brand Awareness and Sentiment:** Use surveys, social media listening tools, and other research methods to track changes in brand awareness, perception, and preference over time. Monitor how your marketing campaigns impact these metrics and adjust your strategies accordingly.

- **ROI:** Measure the ROI of specific marketing initiatives by comparing their costs to the incremental sales and profits they generate. Use this data to prioritize high-performing tactics and optimize your marketing mix.

- **Distributor and Retailer Feedback:** Regularly solicit feedback from your distributor and retailer partners on the effectiveness of your marketing efforts. Ask for their input on what's working, what's not, and how you can better support their needs. Use these insights to strengthen your partnerships and drive better results.

By consistently tracking these metrics and using data to guide your decisions, you can ensure that your marketing efforts are driving meaningful results and contributing to the long-term success of your brand.

7.7 Conclusion—Mastering the Art and Science of Three-Tier Marketing

As we've explored throughout this chapter, marketing within the three-tier system is both an art and a science. It requires a unique blend of creativity, strategic thinking, and regulatory savvy to build a strong, memorable brand that resonates with consumers and drives long-term success.

The key to mastering this complex landscape lies in understanding the unique challenges and opportunities that exist within the three-tier system. By developing a deep knowledge of the regulatory framework, crafting compliant and engaging brand activation strategies, leveraging distributor resources, and creating integrated marketing campaigns that span all three tiers, you can position your brand for success in this dynamic industry.

But success in three-tier marketing isn't just about tactics and strategies; it's also about building strong, collaborative relationships with your distributor and retailer partners. By fostering open communication, aligning around shared goals, and working together to create value for all stakeholders, you can amplify your impact and drive better results.

As you navigate the ever-changing world of alcohol marketing, remember to stay agile, adaptable, and focused on your core brand values. Embrace new technologies and platforms that allow you to connect with consumers in meaningful ways, but never lose sight of the importance of regulatory compliance and responsible marketing practices.

By combining the art of creative storytelling with the science of data-driven decision-making, and by staying true to your brand's unique identity and purpose, you can build a powerful, enduring brand that stands the test of time.

CHAPTER 8

Financial Considerations

8.1 Introduction–The Importance of Strategic Pricing in the Three-Tier System

Welcome to the complex world of financial considerations in the three-tier system. At the heart of this complex landscape lies pricing strategy—a critical factor that can determine a brand's success or failure. In this chapter, we'll delve into the nuances of pricing across the tiers of suppliers, distributors, and retailers, exploring how to develop effective strategies that ensure profitability, support brand positioning, and drive market penetration.

As someone who has navigated pricing strategies for both large and small brands, I've witnessed firsthand the profound impact that well-crafted pricing can have on a brand's trajectory. From balancing production costs and desired margins to managing promotional discounts and adapting to market changes, navigating the art and science of pricing in the alcohol industry is a multifaceted challenge that requires strategic thinking and a deep understanding of the three-tier system.

In the pages ahead, we'll unravel the complexities of pricing in this unique landscape, providing you with the insights and tools needed to develop a pricing strategy that sets your brand up for long-term success. So, let's explore the key elements of financial success in the three-tier system and equip you with the knowledge you need to make informed pricing decisions.

8.2. Understanding Pricing across the Three Tiers

To effectively navigate pricing in the alcohol industry, it's essential to understand the unique considerations and challenges faced by each tier of the three-tier system.

8.2.1 First Tier (Supplier) Pricing Strategies

As a supplier, your pricing strategy lays the foundation for your product's journey through the three-tier system. When setting prices, you must account for production costs and desired profit margins, and leave room for distributor and retailer markups. It's crucial to consider how your pricing will impact your brand's perception and competitive positioning once it reaches the store shelves.

8.2.2 Second Tier (Distributor) Pricing Considerations

Distributors typically operate on a margin basis, adding their markup to the supplier's price. Their pricing must cover operational costs, sales force expenses, and their own profit margins, while keeping the product competitive for retailers. Understanding distributor margin expectations is key for suppliers when setting initial prices.

8.2.3 Third Tier (Retailer) Pricing Dynamics

Retailers have the final say in pricing to consumers, but their decisions are influenced by the prices set by suppliers and distributors. They must balance profitability with consumer price expectations and competitive pressures. As a supplier, understanding retail pricing dynamics, including retailer margin requirements, can help you better position your product for success.

8.3 Developing an Effective Pricing Strategy

Crafting an effective pricing strategy in the alcohol industry involves considering various approaches and understanding their strengths and challenges.

- **Cost-Based Pricing:** This straightforward approach starts with production costs and adds desired profit margins. While it ensures that costs are covered, it may not always align with market realities or consumer perceptions of value.

- **Value-Based Pricing:** This strategy sets prices based on the perceived value to the customer, making it effective for premium or unique products where quality and brand prestige justify higher prices.

- **Competitive Pricing:** Setting prices in relation to competitors can be useful for new market entrants or maintaining market share in competitive categories. However, it's crucial to avoid unsustainable price wars.

ffective pricing strategies blend these approaches,
uction costs, brand value, and the competitive
nsuring that the strategy works across all three tiers.

8.4 Supplier Pricing Models

Suppliers must understand various pricing models to effectively navigate the three-tier system:

- **FOB Pricing:** The supplier sets a price for the product at their warehouse, and the distributor is responsible for transportation costs.

- **Delivered Pricing:** The supplier sets a price that includes delivery to the distributor's warehouse, providing more control over pricing throughout the tiers.

- **Price Posting and Minimum Pricing Laws:** Many states require suppliers to "post" prices with the state alcohol board, and some have minimum pricing laws to prevent below-cost sales.

8.5 Managing Margins across Tiers

Successfully managing margins across all three tiers is crucial for creating a pricing strategy that works for everyone in the supply chain while delivering value to consumers. Typical margin expectations vary:

- **Suppliers:** 50–70 percent gross margin, covering production costs, marketing, sales support, and product development.

- **Distributors:** 25–30 percent for wine and spirits, 25–35 percent for beer, covering operational costs, warehousing, delivery, and sales force expenses.

- **Retailers:** 30–50 percent gross margin, with premium products often commanding higher margins to cover overhead, rent, staff, and inventory costs.

Balancing profitability and competitiveness across these tiers is key, considering factors such as product category, brand prestige, and local market conditions.

8.6 Promotional Pricing and Discounts

Promotional pricing, when used judiciously, can be a powerful tool for driving sales and gaining market share. Common promotions in the alcohol industry include:

- **Temporary Price Reductions (TPRs):** Drive short-term sales volume, often used for new product introductions or clearing excess inventory.

- **Volume Discounts or Quantity Discounts (QDs):** Incentivize larger orders from distributors or retailers, helping to secure shelf space or prominent placements.

- **Holiday or Seasonal Promotions:** Capture sales during peak consumption periods that align with consumer purchasing patterns.

It's essential to ensure that promotional strategies comply with state and federal regulations, as some states prohibit certain practices like below-cost sales or restrict QDs.

8.7 Inventory Management across Tiers

Effective inventory management requires close coordination across all three tiers to balance production, distribution, and retail inventory. Suppliers must work with distributors to understand their inventory needs and adjust production accordingly, preventing out-of-stocks and excess inventory, both of which can negatively impact pricing and profitability.

Accurate forecasting and demand planning are essential, taking into account historical sales data, upcoming promotions, and seasonal trends. This helps maintain pricing stability and ensures consistent product availability.

8.8 Pricing for Different Channels

Crafting an effective pricing strategy requires a nuanced approach that considers the unique characteristics of each sales channel:

- **On-Premise Accounts:** Typically, these command higher margins due to the service and experience provided. Strategic pricing might involve discounts or incentives for menu placements or features to boost brand exposure and encourage consumer trial.

- **Off-Premise Independent Retailers:** Often being more open to new or niche products makes these valuable partners for brands entering the market or expanding their presence. Pricing should balance competitiveness and healthy retailer margins, potentially offering promotional pricing or volume discounts for larger orders and prominent shelf placement.

- **Retail Chains:** These offer the lowest margins but the highest volume potential, requiring particularly competitive pricing due to high consumer price sensitivity. Focus on volume sales and consider volume-based incentives for larger orders and better shelf positioning.

Maintaining price consistency across channels, developing channel-specific stock-keeping units (SKUs) or packaging, and considering cross-channel dynamics are crucial elements of a successful pricing strategy.

8.9 Adapting Pricing Strategies to Market Changes

The alcohol market is dynamic, and successful brands must be prepared to adapt their pricing strategies in response to changing conditions:

- **Competitive Pressures:** While it can be tempting to match or beat competitor prices, it's essential to consider the long-term implications and avoid unsustainable price wars that damage brand equity and erode profitability.

- **Economic Factors:** Recessions or changes in disposable income may necessitate pricing adjustments to maintain market share. During economic downturns, brands may need to offer better value to retain customers without sacrificing too much profitability.

Regularly reviewing and adjusting pricing strategies based on market feedback, sales data, and changing business objectives is crucial for long-term success.

8.10 Conclusion—The Role of Pricing in Brand Success

Setting effective pricing is a delicate balancing act, requiring a deep understanding of costs, brand positioning, competitors, and the unique dynamics of the three-tier system. The most successful alcohol brands view pricing as a strategic tool, continually refining their approach based on market feedback and changing conditions.

Pricing is not just about numbers; it's a reflection of a brand's value proposition, a key driver of relationships with distributors and retailers, and a critical factor in consumer perception and engagement. By approaching pricing with a strategic mindset and a willingness to adapt, brands can navigate the complexities of the three-tier system and build long-term success in the ever-changing alcohol industry.

CHAPTER 9

Looking Ahead–Emerging Trends and Future Predictions for the Alcohol Industry

9.1 Introduction–The Ever-Evolving Landscape of the Alcohol Industry

As we approach the end of our comprehensive exploration of the three-tier system, it's important to acknowledge the ever-changing nature of the alcohol industry. In the previous chapters, we've delved into the complexities of navigating the regulatory landscape, developing a strong brand strategy, and mastering the challenges and opportunities of each tier. Now, we'll focus on the emerging trends and predictions that will shape the alcohol industry in the years to come.

As someone who has witnessed numerous changes and innovations in the industry over the past two decades, I can attest to the fact that the alcohol business is constantly evolving. From the rise of craft beer and spirits to the growing importance of e-commerce and DTC sales, the industry has undergone a significant transformation in recent years, and this pace of change is likely to continue.

In this chapter, we'll examine some of the key trends and predictions that are poised to reshape the alcohol industry in the coming years. We'll explore how technological advancements, changing consumer preferences, and regulatory shifts are creating new opportunities and challenges for suppliers, and we'll discuss strategies for staying informed and adaptable in this ever-changing landscape.

So, let's take a closer look at the future of the alcohol industry and consider how these trends may impact your business strategies moving forward.

9.2 Technological Advancements and Their Impact on the Three-Tier System

One of the most significant drivers of change in the alcohol industry is the rapid pace of technological innovation. From artificial intelligence (AI) and machine learning to blockchain and the Internet of Things, emerging technologies are transforming every aspect of the business, from production and distribution to marketing and sales.

For suppliers, these technological advancements present both opportunities and challenges. On the one hand, new technologies can help streamline operations, reduce costs, and improve efficiency throughout the supply chain. For example, the use of data analytics and predictive modeling can help suppliers better forecast demand, optimize inventory management, and make more informed pricing and promotional decisions.

On the other hand, the adoption of new technologies can also disrupt traditional business models and create new competitors in the market. The rise of e-commerce and DTC sales, for instance, has challenged the traditional three-tier system and given rise to new players in the industry, such as online retailers and subscription services.

To stay ahead of the curve, suppliers must embrace innovation and be willing to experiment with new technologies and business models. This may involve investing in new tools and platforms, partnering with technology providers, or even developing their own proprietary solutions. By staying at the forefront of technological change, suppliers can gain a competitive edge and position themselves for success in the years to come.

9.3 Changing Consumer Preferences and the Rise of New Product Categories

Another major trend shaping the future of the alcohol industry is the shifting preferences and behaviors of consumers. In recent years, we've seen a significant shift toward premiumization, with consumers increasingly seeking out high-quality, craft, and artisanal products. This trend has given rise to a proliferation of new product categories, such as craft beer, small-batch spirits, and natural wines.

At the same time, consumers are becoming more health-conscious and environmentally aware, leading to a growing demand for low-alcohol and non-alcoholic beverages, as well as organic and sustainable products. This trend has created new opportunities for suppliers to innovate and differentiate their offerings, while also posing challenges for traditional brands that may struggle to adapt to changing consumer tastes.

To stay relevant in this evolving landscape, suppliers must keep a close eye on consumer trends and be willing to innovate and experiment with new product offerings. This may involve developing new brands and line extensions, partnering with emerging categories and producers, or investing in research and development to create products that meet the changing needs and preferences of consumers.

9.4 The Growing Importance of E-commerce and DTC Sales

Perhaps the most significant trend reshaping the alcohol industry in recent years has been the rapid growth of e-commerce and DTC sales. With the rise of online shopping and home delivery, consumers are increasingly turning to digital channels to purchase their favorite beverages, bypassing the traditional three-tier system altogether.

For suppliers, the growth of e-commerce and DTC sales presents both opportunities and challenges. On the one hand, these channels offer a new way to reach consumers directly, build brand loyalty, and gather valuable data on consumer preferences and behaviors. On the other hand, the rise of online sales has created new complexities around regulation, taxation, and distribution, as well as increased competition from new players in the market.

To succeed in this new landscape, suppliers must develop a comprehensive e-commerce and DTC strategy that complements their traditional distribution channels. This may involve partnering with established online retailers, developing their own e-commerce platforms, or experimenting with new models such as subscription services or personalized recommendations.

Suppliers must also navigate the complex web of regulations surrounding online alcohol sales, which can vary widely by state and even by locality. By staying informed about the latest regulatory developments and working closely with legal and compliance experts, suppliers can ensure that their e-commerce and DTC efforts are fully compliant and avoid costly penalties or legal challenges.

9.5 Regulatory Changes and Their Potential Impact on the Industry

The alcohol industry is one of the most heavily regulated sectors of the economy, and the regulatory landscape is constantly evolving. In recent years, we've seen a number of significant regulatory changes that have had a major impact on the industry, from the legalization of cannabis in some states to the loosening of restrictions on DTC shipping.

Looking ahead, there are a number of regulatory trends and developments that suppliers will need to keep a close eye on. One major area of focus is the ongoing debate over the three-tier system itself, with some advocates calling for a more flexible and modernized approach to alcohol distribution. While the three-tier system is likely to remain in place for the foreseeable future, suppliers should be prepared for potential changes and disruptions to the status quo.

Another area of regulatory concern is the increasing focus on public health and social responsibility, with governments and advocacy groups seeking to reduce the negative impacts of alcohol consumption on individuals and communities. This trend could lead to new restrictions on alcohol advertising and marketing, as well as increased taxes and other measures aimed at curbing excessive drinking.

To navigate this complex and ever-changing regulatory landscape, suppliers must stay informed about the latest developments and work closely with industry associations, legal experts, and other stakeholders to ensure compliance and mitigate risk. By proactively engaging with regulators and policymakers, suppliers can also help shape the future of the industry and advocate for policies that support their long-term growth and success.

9.6 Strategies for Suppliers to Stay Ahead of the Curve and Thrive in the Future

As the alcohol industry continues to evolve and transform, suppliers must be proactive and adaptable to stay ahead of the curve and thrive in the years to come. Here are a few key strategies that suppliers can employ to position themselves for success:

- **Embrace Innovation and Experimentation:** In a rapidly changing industry, suppliers must be willing to take risks and try new things. This may involve investing in new technologies, developing new products and brands, and/or experimenting with new business models and distribution channels.

- **Focus on Quality and Differentiation:** With consumers increasingly seeking out unique and high-quality products, suppliers must focus on crafting distinctive and memorable offerings that stand out in a crowded market. This may involve sourcing premium ingredients, employing innovative production techniques, and/or telling compelling brand stories that resonate with consumers.

- **Build Strong Partnerships and Collaborations:** In an increasingly complex and competitive industry, suppliers can't go it alone. Building strong partnerships and collaborations with distributors, retailers, technology providers, and other stakeholders can help suppliers access new markets, share knowledge and resources, and create value for all parties involved.

- **Prioritize Data and Analytics:** In the era of big data and AI, suppliers must prioritize the collection, analysis, and application of data to inform their decision-making and strategy. By leveraging data on consumer preferences, market trends, and product performance, suppliers can optimize their operations, personalize their marketing efforts, and identify new growth opportunities.

- **Invest in Talent and Culture:** As the industry evolves, so too must the skills and capabilities of the workforce. Suppliers must invest in attracting, developing, and retaining top talent, as well as fostering a culture of innovation, collaboration, and continuous learning. By building a strong and adaptable team, suppliers can navigate the challenges and opportunities of the future with confidence and resilience.

9.7 Conclusion—Embracing Change and Building a Thriving Brand in the Three-Tier System

As we've seen throughout this chapter, the alcohol industry is in the midst of a profound transformation, driven by technological advancements, changing consumer preferences, and regulatory shifts. For suppliers, this transformation presents both challenges and opportunities, and the key to success lies in the ability to adapt, innovate, and stay ahead of the curve.

By embracing the strategies and mindset outlined in this chapter, suppliers can position themselves for long-term growth and success in the three-tier system. Whether it's investing in new technologies and business models, crafting distinctive and high-quality products, building strong partnerships and collaborations, or leveraging data and analytics to inform decision-making, the most successful suppliers will be those who are proactive, agile, and always looking toward the future.

As we conclude our in-depth exploration of the three-tier system, I encourage you to reflect on the insights and lessons we've covered throughout this book. From understanding the regulatory landscape and developing a strong brand strategy to navigating the challenges and opportunities of each tier, we've explored the key elements of building a successful brand in the alcohol industry.

However, your work as a brand owner doesn't stop here. As the industry continues to evolve and change, so too must your approach and strategy. By staying informed, adaptable, and committed to continuous learning, you can build a brand that not only survives but thrives in the complex and competitive world of alcohol distribution.

CHAPTER 10

Conclusion—A Roadmap to Success

10.1 Recapping the Journey through the Three-Tier System

Congratulations on making it to the end of our journey through the complex and fascinating world of the three-tier system! Throughout this book, we've explored the intricacies of the alcohol industry, uncovering the challenges, opportunities, and strategies for success at every step of the way.

From understanding the historical context and regulatory landscape of the three-tier system to mastering the art of brand-building, distribution, and retail sales, we've covered a wide range of topics that are essential for any supplier looking to thrive in this dynamic industry. We've delved into the unique characteristics of each tier, examined best practices for navigating the competitive landscape, and discussed the importance of building strong relationships with key stakeholders.

As we've seen, the alcohol industry is not for the faint-hearted. It requires a deep understanding of the regulatory environment, a strategic approach to brand positioning and marketing, a keen eye for financial management and pricing, and a willingness to adapt to changing market conditions and consumer preferences. But for those who are passionate, persistent, and always learning, the rewards of building a successful brand in the three-tier system are immeasurable.

In this final chapter, we'll recap the key takeaways from each section of the book, providing you with a clear and concise roadmap for implementing the strategies and best practices we've discussed. We'll also explore a framework for success that you can use to assess your current position in the market, identify areas for improvement, and chart a course for long-term growth and profitability.

So, let's raise a glass to your future success and dive into the conclusion of our journey through the three-tier system.

10.2 Key Takeaways from Each Chapter

Throughout this book, we've covered a wide range of topics that are essential for success in the alcohol industry. Here are the key takeaways from each chapter:

10.2.1 Understanding the Three-Tier System and Its Regulatory Landscape

- The three-tier system was established after Prohibition to prevent vertical integration and promote a fair, competitive market for alcohol sales.

- The system consists of three distinct tiers—producers, distributors, and retailers—each with its own unique roles and responsibilities.

- Navigating the complex web of federal, state, and local regulations is essential for compliance and success in the industry.

10.2.2 Developing a Strong Brand Strategy

- A strong brand strategy is the foundation for success in the alcohol industry, differentiating your products and creating a loyal customer base.

- Key elements of a successful brand strategy include defining your USP, developing a compelling brand story and visual identity, and understanding your target market and competitive landscape.

- Effective brand positioning and marketing requires a deep understanding of your distribution channels and a willingness to adapt to changing market conditions and consumer preferences.

10.2.3 Navigating the Challenges and Opportunities of Each Tier

- The first tier, production, requires a focus on quality, consistency, and efficiency, as well as a strong understanding of your cost structure and pricing strategy.

- The second tier, distribution, is all about building strong relationships with wholesalers, leveraging their expertise and resources, and ensuring that your products are well-represented in the market.

- The third tier, retail, requires a deep understanding of your target consumers, a strategic approach to pricing and promotions, and a focus on building strong relationships with key accounts.

10.2.4 Implementing Effective Marketing and Pricing Strategies

- Effective marketing in the three-tier system requires a combination of brand activation, distributor partnerships, and retail promotions, all while staying compliant with complex regulations.

- Pricing strategies must take into account the unique dynamics of each tier, balancing margin requirements with competitive pressures and consumer expectations.

- Successful suppliers use data and analytics to inform their marketing and pricing decisions, continually monitoring and adapting to changes in the market.

By understanding and applying these key takeaways, you'll be well-equipped to navigate the challenges and seize the opportunities of the three-tier system, and to build a strong and profitable brand that stands the test of time.

10.3 A Framework for Success—Action Steps for Suppliers

Knowing the key strategies and best practices is one thing; putting them into action is another. To help you translate the insights from this book into tangible results for your business, here's a simple framework you can use to assess your current position, identify areas for improvement, and chart a course for success:

- **Assess Your Current Position in the Market:** Take a step back and honestly evaluate your brand's strengths, weaknesses, opportunities, and threats. Consider factors such as your product quality, brand reputation, distribution footprint, pricing strategy, and competitive landscape.

- **Define Your Brand Identity and Value Proposition:** Clearly articulate what makes your brand unique and compelling to your target consumers. Develop a strong brand story and visual identity that reflects your values and resonates with your audience.

- **Build Strong Relationships with Distributors and Retailers:** Invest time and resources in cultivating strong, mutually beneficial partnerships with your distribution and retail partners. Understand their needs and priorities, and work collaboratively to achieve shared goals.

- **Develop a Flexible and Adaptive Marketing and Pricing Strategy:** Create a marketing plan that leverages the unique opportunities of each tier, from brand activation and distributor promotions to retail merchandising and consumer engagement. Develop a pricing strategy that balances margin requirements with competitive pressures and consumer expectations, and be willing to adapt to changing market conditions.

- **Stay Informed about Industry Trends and Regulatory Changes:** Keep a close eye on the latest developments in the alcohol industry, from evolving consumer preferences and emerging product categories to regulatory updates and legal challenges. Attend industry events, read trade publications, and engage with peers and experts to stay ahead of the curve.

By following this framework and continually assessing and adapting your strategies, you'll be well-positioned to build a successful brand that navigates the complexities of the three-tier system with confidence and skill.

10.4 Closing Thoughts—Embracing Change and Building a Thriving Brand in the Three-Tier System

As we've seen throughout this book, the alcohol industry is a dynamic, ever-changing landscape that requires suppliers to be nimble, strategic, and always learning. From the regulatory complexities of the three-tier system to the evolving preferences of consumers and the rapid pace of technological change, there's no shortage of challenges and opportunities for those looking to build a successful brand in this industry.

But with challenge comes opportunity, and, for those who are willing to put in the work, stay curious, and adapt to change, the rewards of building a thriving brand in the alcohol industry are immense. Whether you're a small craft producer just starting out or a large established brand looking to expand your reach, the strategies and insights we've covered in this book will help you navigate the complexities of the three-tier system with confidence and skill.

As you embark on your own journey of building a prosperous alcohol brand, remember that the key to success lies not just in the strategies and tactics you employ but in the mindset and approach you bring to the table. Embrace change as an opportunity to learn and grow, stay focused on delivering value to your customers and partners, and never lose sight of the passion and purpose that drove you to enter this industry in the first place.

Building a prosperous brand in the alcohol industry is not a destination; it's a journey—one that requires hard work, dedication, and a willingness to adapt and evolve. But with the right knowledge, tools, and mindset, you have everything you need to succeed in this challenging and competitive industry.

So, here's to your success, and to the many opportunities that await you in the complex world of alcohol distribution. May you always stay curious, stay passionate, and stay committed to building a brand that delivers value to your consumers and stands the test of time.

Cheers!

—Dave

APPENDIX—Useful Resour(

Industry Associations and Trade Groups

- American Craft Spirits Association (ACSA): https://americancraftspirits.org

- American Distilled Spirits Alliance (ADSA): www.distilledspirits.org

- Brewers Association: www.brewersassociation.org

- National Beer Wholesalers Association (NBWA): www.nbwa.org

- Wine Institute: https://wineinstitute.org

- Wine & Spirits Wholesalers of America (WSWA): www.wswa.org

Regulatory Bodies and Information Sources

- Alcohol and Tobacco Tax and Trade Bureau (TTB): www.ttb.gov

- Code of Federal Regulations (CFR) Title 27—Alcohol, Tobacco Products, and Firearms: www.ecfr.gov/current/title-27

National Alcohol Beverage Control Association (NABCA): www.nabca.org

- National Conference of State Liquor Administrators (NCSLA): www.ncsla.org

Educational Resources and Training Programs

- American Brewers Guild: www.abgbrew.com

- Cicerone Certification Program: www.cicerone.org

- Napa Valley Wine Academy: https://napavalleywineacademy.com

- Society of Wine Educators: www.societyofwineeducators.org

- University of California Davis Extension—Winemaking Certificate Program: https://extension.ucdavis.edu/areas-study/winemaking

- Wine & Spirit Education Trust (WSET): www.wsetglobal.com

Industry Publications and News Sources

- Craft Brewing Business: www.craftbrewingbusiness.com/

- Decanter: www.decanter.com

- Distiller Magazine: https://distilling.com/distillermagazine

- Drinks Business: www.thedrinksbusiness.com

- SevenFifty Daily: https://daily.sevenfifty.com
- Shanken News Daily: www.shankennewsdaily.com
- SOMM Journal: www.sommjournal.com
- Tasting Panel Magazine: www.tastingpanelmag.com
- Wine Spectator: www.winespectator.com
- Wine Enthusiast Magazine: www.winemag.com

E-commerce and DTC Platforms

- Minibar Delivery: https://minibardelivery.com
- ReserveBar: www.reservebar.com
- Speakeasy Co.: www.speakeasyco.com
- Thirstie: https://thirstie.com
- Wine.com: www.wine.com

Data and Analytics Resources

- Circana: www.circana.com/industry-expertise/alcoholic-beverages
- Dimensional Insight: www.dimins.com
- IWSR (formerly International Wine and Spirits Record): www.theiwsr.com
- Nielsen: www.nielsen.com
- SipSource: www.wswa.org/sipsource

Made in the USA
Monee, IL
15 January 2025